OLD AND NEW WORLD LYRICS

BY

CLINTON SCOLLARD

Author of "With Reed and Lyre"

NEW YORK
FREDERICK A. STOKES & BROTHER
MDCCCLXXXVIII

TO MY FATHER.

CONTENTS.

FROM OVER SEAS.

	PAGE
Sidney Godolphin	1
At the Grave of Keats	4
The Banquet of Sir Reginald	7
VENETIAN BAS-RELIEFS.	
From the Campanile	12
The Feeding of the Doves	14
Achille	16
On the Grand Canal	25
The Doge's Well	27
Artist and Friar	29
In the Boboli Gardens	31
At Certosa	33
Fiesole	35
Maggiore	37
The Maid of the Trevi Fountain	39
The Catacombs	41
Paestum	42
The Sentinel of Lucerne	44

PAGE

The Monk of Rapperschwyl 46
The Sword 49
In England 52
A Yachting Song 54
Ghosts 56
In the Cathedral at Cologne 57
EASTERN POEMS.
From Helouan 59
A Kaffeyeh 61
Moonlight in the Orient 63
Ascalon. 65
The Grotto of Pan 67
Baalbec. 70
Princess Badoura 72
A Bit of Marble 75
From Pentelicus 76
The Mænads 78
Orpheus 80
The Crucifix 82
A Twilight Piece 102

THE SEASONS ROUND.

Carmen Hiemis. 109
An April Song. 113

PAGE

A May Carol 115
A June Harmony 117
A Midsummer Harbinger 120
As August Comes 122
As Wanes the Year in Autumn-tide . . 123
In Late November 125
Beside the Ingle 127

SONNETS AND QUATRAINS.

From the Castle Terrace 131
Paris Revisited 132
First Sight of Rome 133
The Bay of Naples 134
A Damascus Picture 135
Summer Noon 136
A Pearl 137
The Statue 138
The Mendicant 139
Wheat 140
The Actor 141
Marble 141
Icicles 141
Milkweed 142
Diamonds 142

HOME SONGS.

	PAGE
The Rocky Mountains	145
Moonrise at Monterey	147
A Serenade	148
The Prodigals	150
Our Saint	153
In Solitude	156
The Bric-à-Brac Shop	157
Harebells	159
An African Lily	160
A Rose	161
A Winter Twilight	162
Mellona	164
In the Park	166
Nightfall	169
A Dream of Peace	170

SIDNEY GODOLPHIN.

THEY rode from the camp at morn
With clash of sword and spur,
The birds were loud in the thorn,
The sky was an azure blur.
A gallant show they made
That warm noon-tide of the year,
Led on by a dashing blade,
By the poet-cavalier.

They laughed through the leafy lanes,
The long lanes of Dartmoor ;
And they sang their soldier strains,
Pledged "death" to the Roundhead boor ;
Then they came at the middle day
To a hamlet quaint and brown
Where the hated troopers lay,
And they cheered for the King and crown.

They fought in the fervid heat,
Fought fearlessly and well,
But low at the foeman's feet
Their valorous leader fell.
Full on his fair young face
The blinding sun beat down ;
In the morn of his manly grace
He died for the King and crown.

O the pitiless blow,
The vengance-thrust of strife,
That blotted the golden glow
From the sky of his glad, brave life !
The glorious promise gone ;—
Night with its grim black frown !
Never again the dawn,
And all for the King and crown.

Hidden his sad fate now
In the sealèd book of the years ;
Few are the heads that bow,
Or the eyes that brim with tears,

Reading 'twixt blots and stains
From a musty tome that saith
How he rode through the Dartmoor lanes
To his woeful, dauntless death.

But I, in the summer's prime,
From that lovely leafy land
Look back to the olden time
And the leal and loyal band.
I see them dash along,—
I hear them charge and cheer,
And my heart goes out in a song
To the poet-cavalier.

AT THE GRAVE OF KEATS.

'TWAS in the heart of purple vintage-time,
The mellow season that he loved so well,
I wandered out at early vesper-chime.
Rome had cast off the summer's torrid spell,
And in the air
Moved a kind coolness, from the mountains blown,
Across the billowy zone
The wide Campagna makes around the throne
Where sits the city, still supremely fair.

Through long and winding ways at last I came
To memory-sacred, sadly-hallowed ground,
And there my yearning eyes beheld his name.
There was a haunting, tender silence round,
Save for the cries
Of happy blind boys in a field at play,
More innocently gay
Than many an one who looks upon the day
With never clouded, all-discerning eyes.

A rose hedge bloomed along a sheltering wall;
    And dying wafts of summer, soft exhaled,
Were borne from petals, trembling to the fall.
    Then, while the great sun's glorv slowly failed,
    And softly stirred
In sound articulate each cypress tree,
I thought, O ecstacy,
If from yon sombre bough-top, wild and free,
    Could drop the nightingale's clear word on word!

In vain, in vain! The birds, if there, were mute,
    As if somehow their gentle spirits knew
Those lips so silent 'neath the sod's fine root
    Once sang their praise that rings remote lands
        through.
    A laurel's leaves,
As green as is his fame, above the mould
That doth his dust enfold,
Gave him the crown, that, after life is cold,
    The world with tardy hand so often weaves.

Ah, grave of graves! what pathos round it clings!
    To this sad bourne from coming age to age,

While the tired earth endures its sufferings,
Will wandering feet make worship's pilgrimage !
Thou, hoary Rome,
In bosoming him hast higher glory won,
Although for Pantheon
Thou gav'st him naught, save that wherein the sun
Beams morn by morn, an everlasting dome.

Before I turned I plucked a laurel spray
For fond remembrance-token. Night unfurled
Her spectral wings, and vague and vast and gray
Grew the great void above the restless world.
But bright afar,
Ere yet were friendly portals open thrown,
From out the dim unknown,
Athwart my heaven-uplifted vision shone
Adown a luminous path, one splendid star !

THE BANQUET OF SIR REGINALD.

NIGHT on the walls of the castle, and night in
the streets of the town
Night in the aisles of the forest, and night on the
wastes of the down ;
Night with the clamor of winds and the heaven's most
ominous frown.

Never a gleam of a star in a sky that is boding and
black,
Never a beam from the moon sailing slow up her
silvery track,
Never a break in the gloom of the leaden and dolorous
wrack.

Rain in thin wreaths that are tossed by the blast as it
fitfully blows,
Rain such as steadily falls at the flight of the last
winter snows,
Rain in wild torrents that madden the peacefullest
streamlet that flows.

Lights in the court of the castle,—behold, in the feasting hall, light!
Flashes of flame on the armor so brilliantly burnished and bright,
Laughter and jest on the lip,—for Sir Reginald banquets to-night.

Reginald, bold in the tourney, the first and the last in the field;
Reginald, mighty of arm, and the cleaver of helmet and shield;
Reginald, last of the line of the crest blazoned, "Never to yield."

Merry the hearts of the guests, for the wine has flowed freely around;
Drunk are the healths of the maidens that nature with beauty has crowned.
"Hark ye!" cries Reginald, rising; and lo! not a breath at the sound.

Flushed is his face with the fruity red vintage so freely
outpoured ;
Forth from its sheath at his side leaps the glittering
blade of his sword ;
Loudly it rings as he dashes it down on the banqueting
board.

" Men call me scoffer," he sneers, "and my deeds by
the priests are abhorred.
Why should I rail at their Christ, who taught living in
loving accord ?
Down on your knees where ye are ; we will have the
last feast of the Lord !"

Pallid the face of each guest as he kneels at the blas-
phemous sign.
Bearing a trencher of bread and a flagon o'erbrimming
with wine,
Sneering, Sir Reginald passeth along down the suppli-
ant line.

Waver the lights in the hall, and a sound smites the
hush of the air,
Awful with rushing of pinions unseen in the glimmer
and glare,
While through the night pierce the shrieks of a soul in
the hell of despair.

Trencher and flagon are dashed to the floor, and Sir
Reginald reels ;
Loud from his agonized lips through the halls of the
castle there peals
That which the terrified heart of a coward and craven
reveals.

Forward he falls with an outcry that dies to a pitiful
moan ;
Tremble the walls of the castle, and quiver the turrets
of stone,
Swaying like trees in the grasp of a hurricane shaken
and blown.

Forth through the torrents that pour as the floods at
the equinox fall,
Haunted to madness by omens of dread that their
spirits appall,
Rush in their terror the banqueters, fleeing the doom-
stricken hall.

Night on the wastes of the down, and the tempest's
tumultuous breath
Voicing the horror abroad with the tongue of the whirl-
wind that saith,
"Death in the courts of the castle, grim silence and
darkness and death!"

FROM THE CAMPANILE.

BATHED in the glow of golden morning light,
  And shining with the sheen of varied dyes
A domèd marvel to the dazzled sight,
  Venice beneath me lies.

The Doge's massive palace walls I see
  I see St. Mark's in orient glory shine ;
And on its front in antique symmetry
  The steeds of Constantine.

Mute slaves of Time, the sledge-armed giants keep
  Their sombre ward where straight the Bell-Tower
      springs ;
And o'er the Piazzetta's sunny sweep
  The Lion lifts its wings.

The soft lights change upon lagoons afar
From deepest blue to gray and emerald pale ;
And veering lazily by bank and bar,
Strange-pinioned vessels sail.

Is it a dream,—a mirage of the brain
That some fantastic Merlin-spell has wrought,
A vision that dissolves and forms again
With all the speed of thought ?

No ! nothing fades ; still floods the lustrous light,
Still wide expands the arch of peerless skies,
And still, a marvel to the dazzled sight,
Venice beneath me lies.

THE FEEDING OF THE DOVES.

WITH heat was the air aswoon,
      Not the ghost of a breeze was astir,
When a great bell clamored noon,
      And there came the flutter and whir
Of doves sailing softly down
To the square in Venice-town.

That kindly hour they knew
      By the deep, reiterant sound ;
And fearlessly down they flew,
      And gathered in gladness round
Where a generous hand they spied
That scattered the kernels wide.

Then beamingly out of the throng
      Ran a fair little maiden, gay ;
Her laugh was a whole sweet song,
      Her look was a loving ray.

There was corn in her palm outspread,
And a white dove lit and fed.

What a perfect scene of peace !
  In Venice peace: no more
The Austrian's insolent ease
  By the Adriatic's shore ;
But peace where the blue skies be,
Over an Italy free !

ACHILLE.

(Scene—A hospital in Venice. Achille and a priest.
Achille speaks.)

ACHILLE am I called. I dwell alone
Upon a sinuous street that blindly ends
Behind the Redentore. High above
The grass-grown pavement of the silent square
I have my humble lodgment. I am known
To few who in that squalid quarter house,
But honest-hearted merchants that anigh
The holy Frari ply their meagre trade
Can give me good repute. My gondola
Once shot along Venetian water-ways
As fleetly as the swiftest, and no hand
Than mine was defter with the long lithe oar.
But that is past.

"Haste," said you?

With mine eyes
I seemed to catch that word upon your lips,
That word and others, so that now I know
My little lamp of life will soon die out
And darkness close about me. Note you not
How speech eludes my hearing? Mine own voice
Sounds faint, like far off murmur of the waves
At night upon the Lido. Nearer;—stoop!
I would not have you miss one lightest word
Lest missing one, your absolution fail.

How happily together she and I
Dwelt with our laughing, roguish, winsome boy
Whose added summers not yet numbered four!
That was before her cruel father came,
He who had tarried long at Padua
As Ecelino's servile underling.
In that glad time the days with laggard feet
Dragged ever by, till I could get me home,
And feel my fair boy's arms about my neck,
And echo back her smile with kindred joy.
Oft in the quiet of the summer eves

Below some stately, massive palace stair,
While I touched lightly the guitar's sweet strings,
Would she uplift her voice, divinely clear,
And spell the night with rapturous melodies.
And oft have princely ladies overleaned
From balconies silk-screened, soft-praising her,
And oft have nobles from the palace doors
Tossed out a shining disc of orient gold,
And bid her buy some bauble. This was ere
Her cruel father came to bide with us.
Ah ! dark the weeks from that dark hour, until
There came a day, the darkest of them all.

After the mocking profile of his face
First cast upon our wall its evil shade
She never seemed the same. Night following night
I saw her lessening welcome ; faint the smile
That met my warmth of greeting. I, dull fool,
Deemed some slight ailment vexed her ; till one eve,
Incoming early at the darkness' verge,
I heard her father pour within her ear
The subtle poison of a lying tale;—

How I was basely false ; spent idle days
With some soft paramour ; (for then it chanced
The sun of fortune shone not down on me,
And I brought little home for hungry mouths.)
Mad with surprise, stirred by his words so base
To desperate action, I confronted him ;
Then took all caution wings, for when the hound,
Seeing my fury, whimpered cringingly
That he but heard these things low-noised about,
Did not believe them, was but asking her
Could she believe them, I cast back the lie
Into his wicked face, and bade him go
And darken ne'er again a door of mine,
Lest in my anger I should throttle him
And silence evermore his slanderous tongue.
So crept he out, not answering me a word.

And she ? What said she ? Naught. She made no sign
While I was speaking, and when I had done
Only looked at me with her large calm eyes
In mute reproach that was more hard to bear

Than all her father's calumnies. The thought
That ire had made me not quite just to him,
That some malignant knave with malice fine
From pure unblushing wickedness had stilled
This lie, perchance, into the old man's brain,
Brought keen regret to harrow me.

"Forgive,"
I cried repentantly, "forgive me, Love,
I'll bring him back and crave his pardon here."
With that I went.
I sought him near and far
In stifling haunts he frequented by night,
But found him not. "He will come back," I said,
Communing with myself, "the morrow morn;
Or should he not, more easy then my search.
Mayhap e'en now he has returned to beg
My patience with him." Thus I, homeward-bent,
Dreamed blindly of forgiveness mutual.

Now had the night come down,—a dull damp night,
And all the myrmidons of darkness drew

Their mantles o'er the city. Ambushed fear
Leaped sudden out and seemed to strangle me,
When, looking upward, at the accustomed pane
I saw no loving taper. No thick film
Be-dimmed my eyes, for, beaconing through the dark,
Patiently burned a clear flame opposite.
I stumbled onward as a tired man goes
Unguided up a stony slope by night,
And found—black emptiness! The only voice
That answer gave to my beseeching cries
Was mocking echo.
O those pitiless hours,
Those anguished hours until the midnight stormed
The windless silence from an unseen tower!
What awful doubts in grim procession stalked
Throughout my mind, slaying each new-born hope!
What dismal fancies rose and grew and grasped
My strained imagination, till my brain
Reeled to the verge of madness!
Would she come?—
I prayed,—I cried in frenzy unto God,
Upbraiding him. I cursed. Then midnight struck.

The long-reiterant and solemn sound
Aroused again my dazed intelligence,
And as the last stroke dolorously died
I sought the outer world's unlighted gloom.
Swift fell the rain. The chill reviving air
Was grateful to me. On my fevered brow
I let the cool drops fall. Clear grew my thoughts,
And from the night once more I inward turned.
At last sleep came, a phantom-haunted sleep.

I wakened suddenly. A sullen morn
Looked through the casement, and I heard a voice,
His voice, her father's voice. Ah ! how I sprang
Upright with joy, but when I saw his face
I felt joy sicken to a pale despair,
Then die, and quickly nascent in its stead
Came those dire twins, black anger and revenge.
Yet had I held these tigers under curb,
Had not vile venom from his serpent tongue
My wounded bosom poisoned. How he laughed,
And boasted loudly in my very face
That he had lured her from me. To what end

This most unnatural deed had been wrought out
He gave not forth, nor yet divulged he why
Toward me he harbored hatred. Did he think
I had no feeling that he tarried thus
And trifled with my heart-strings?
He had learned
All craft, all crimes, all subtle wickedness
From Ecelino while at Padua;
Yet when I gave that furious panther-spring,
My hot hands itching for his skinny throat,
Of what availed his wiles?
I strangled him
And cast him from me like a vermin rat.
And then———What said you? Trial? Murder? nay!
Venice has haunts that tell no troublous tales,
And who was there to miss him?
She?
Ah! God,
Was this thy ever-sure, just meting-out
Of punishment, that on the next day morn
Below the tide-stained steps that lead adown

From the Salute's holy, hallowed doors
The cruel water should give up its dead?
They found her there, and in her arms our boy,
Our dark-haired boy.
                                        How very cold it grows!
The doctors say this woeful hurt of mine
Is slow in healing. Night has come so soon,
I fear—

Give me your hand!
                                                            'Tis brighter now,
And yet methinks 'tis growing dark again.
Dear Christ, have mercy on my soul!

(The Priest)

Amen!

ON THE GRAND CANAL.

NIGHT had put out the day's refulgent eye ;
I saw a gondolier go gliding by,
And cried at him the clear Venetian cry.

He heard and paused and deftly put to shore
With skillful movement of his long slim oar
That seemed to touch the tide and turn,—no more.

The rippling waves made music in mine ear ;
The Campanile tall gave answer clear
From where it lifted skyward like a spear.

No cloud above us drew its curtain gray ;
A silver girdle gleamed the milky-way ;
" Behold the glory," seemed each star to say.

On toward the city's silent heart we wound ;
Far voices singing sent a dreamy sound
O'er darkling water lapping low around.

In silent, gloomy grandeur overhead
Towered massive records of a glory dead,
Great walls from which the glow of life had fled.

I could but dream how from each door of old,
Proud nobles, clad in scarlet and in gold,
Sailed gaily down the flood that seaward rolled.

And now a stranger and a wanderer, I,
From that broad land beneath the western sky
Sailed as they sailed, but passed in wonder by ;

And thought, when I beheld above me span
The grand Rialto's arch of perfect plan,
"How glorious yet brief the life of man !"

Here stands his work as firm as on the day
The first foot o'er it found a lightsome way,
But ah ! the hands that wrought it, where are they ?

THE DOGE'S WELL.

THIS happy tale Venetian legends tell,
        That he who to the city would return
Must drop a coin within the Doge's Well.

What time lagoons beneath mid-morning burn,
        I sought the great Piazza, still and wide,
Where Time's grim giants sound their mandate stern.

I braved the southern sunlight's glowing tide,
        Till in the shady palace court alone
I leaned upon the broad well's bronzen side.

Then cast I in a tiny metal zone,
        And watched it cut the clear lymph, till it lay
A promise to the hand that erst had thrown.

I flashed a parting glance and took my way
        Back through the lone Piazza. How it all
Comes to my mind once more,—that last bright day!

Around me now the leaves of autumn fall ;
        I mark the sullen reaches of the main
Against the eastern sky, a dull, blank wall.

Shall I not see thy smiling face again,
        O well-beloved Venice ?—Who can tell ?
A thrill of doubt leaps through my heart like pain.

Has it no power, that legendary spell ?
        Will it not one day bid my steps return,
The coin I cast within the Doge's Well ?

ARTIST AND FRIAR.

SHOULD you in Florence wander where
The Past has hoarded riches rare,—
Paintings, within whose perfect lines
The kindling touch of genius shines,
Statues, throughout whose marble limbs
A seeming life-blood leaps and swims,—
Among the names recounted long
With honor in enduring song,
One will be heard where'er you go,
The Master's,—Michael Angelo.

And you will hear another name
Blown by the trumpet-blast of fame
Through Christian lands. No halls of art
Bespeak the throbbings of his heart,
But streets are vocal, and the square
That heard his final martyr-prayer.

A rosary his fingers told,
The cap he wore in cloisters old,
Some blazoned books, are all they show
Of noble Fra Girolamo.

Both long have slumbered in the clay
Yet both are living on to-day.
Time hath no bondage of control
O'er emanations of the soul.
The years have shown how well they wrought,
Preserving still their priceless thought.
One fashioned forms most fair to see,
The other worked intangibly.
The Artist stands as first confessed,
And yet the Friar wrought the best !

IN THE BOBOLI GARDENS.

WHERE statued Plenty lifts on high
Her bearded wheat-spears in the air,
I saw the blue Italian sky
Look down on Florence full and fair.

A transient touch of autumn's gold
Made bright the leaves of many a twig,
And on far slopes that upward rolled
The purple deepened on the fig.

Around the flooding sunlight lay ;
Below a gossip fountain played ;
Above, across the brilliant day,
The statue threw a line of shade.

Along the pathways all was still,
No troublous sound to break the charm ;

And halcyon quiet reigned until
  There came two lovers arm in arm.

The olive flushed upon his cheek
  In listening to her low replies ;
I caught, whene'er she turned to speak,
  The starlight of the Tuscan skies.

And ere they wandered from my sight
  My fancy wove a wayward spell ;
He was her true, faith-plighted knight,
  And she his lady, honored well.

A miracle these lovers wrought
  Soft-whispering of their hopes and fears,
For through my brain had flashed a thought
  That blotted out six hundred years.

AT CERTOSA.

VINE-GIRT the monastery stands
Upon its Tuscan height;
The monks with pale uplifted hands
Make prayer a long delight.

In spotless flowing robes they pass,
Perform their simple deeds,
Rcturning evermore to mass
And holy rosary beads.

As tranquilly the days slip by
As do the beads they tell;—
The morning bird-song in the sky,
The vesper's tolling bell.

Naught know they of the world's keen stress,
The conflict seething round;
Hedged closely in their calm recess
They catch nor sight nor sound.

Yields it the highest good to thus
From mankind dwell apart ?
Can noblest thoughts and generous
Find pathway to the heart ?

The cowl and cassock forth should fare ;
Let earth's broad ways be trod
The deed and not the day-long prayer
Finds surest flight to God.

FIESOLE.

SAY not that Arno's vale is fair,
And Florence fair and good to see
Until from far Fiesole
You view them, bright through cloudless air.

What skies are like Italian skies?
Where do the olive and the vine
With larger wealth of fruitage shine
Than here, beneath the ravished eyes?

Love you not Arno's tawny gold,
Feel you not somehow near akin
To Florence, with her woe and sin
And all the deeds she wrought of old?

How great her gifts! her open heart
Has yielded much to bless mankind,
And in her bosom still we find
A precious treasure-house of art.

And thou, Fiesole, and thou,
    O'er all her glory leaning down,
    With thy serene monastic crown
And morning on thine ancient brow,

Thou art her guardian, smiling sweet
    Upon her, as upon a child
    A mother fond has ever smiled,
Her child at play about her feet.

Keep watchful ward above her still
    With prescience of the vast To-be!
    Look down the years, Fiesole,
From off thy spirit-haunted hill!

MAGGIORE.

FRIEND, rest awhile upon thy glistening oars,
And let us drift and dream
Of naught beyond these mountain-bordered shores
That in the sunlight gleam.

Away, all memory of life's storm and stress,
All thought of days to be !
Hail, holy calm and sweet forgetfulness,
Beloved Italy !

In tiny sapphire ripples round us break
The wavelets, one by one,
Upon the bosom of the fairest lake
That sees the shining sun.

Italian breezes, languorous and low,
Around us steal and sigh ;
From peak to peak, suffused with amber glow,
Spans the Italian sky.

If paradise there be on earthly shores,
  Here is its heavenly gleam.
Then, friend, rest idly on thy dripping oars,
  And let us drift and dream.

THE MAID OF THE TREVI FOUNTAIN.

LITTLE maid by the fountain there,
You with the eyes cast down,
And the cheek of crimsoned brown,
And the unbound raven hair,
And the languorous Roman air ;

What do you do all day?
Do you wistfully stand and stand
With that little dusky hand
Outstretched in a pleading way
For the travelers' *soldi*,—say?

If I go to the basin's brink
O'erlooked by the Neptune old,
(As the legend bids, I'm told ;)
Should I come again, do you think,
If I did but dip and drink?

Should I come and see you here,
  Just a trifle grown may be,
  But still as fair and free
And blithe as you now appear,
This wintry time of the year?

You look, but you do not speak;
  Strange, such a spell you flung,
  I forgot my alien tongue
Must sound in your ears like "Greek,"
Sweet one with the tingèd cheek.

No, I will go my way,
  Nor quaff from the fountain-head,
  Lest coming I find you fled,
And darken the whole bright day
With thoughts that are grim and gray.

Better to dream you fair
  By the Trevi fountain still,
  To dream of you free from ill,
You with your tangled hair,
And your languorous Roman air.

THE CATACOMBS.

AN eddying speck the swallow flies,
The morn is full of fragrant breath,
Yet, dark and dank beneath, there lies
A charnel-house of death.

Spring comes, and straightway at her smiles
The wide Campagna bursts in bloom;
But naught again to life beguiles
The grave's black hecatomb.

And yet the fairest flowers have birth
In mould and darkness and decay;
And here the faith that rings the earth
Flowered into endless day.

PAESTUM.

ACROSS the sea from Sybaris they came,
Oaring their galleys with long sweep and slow,
Those daring Greeks who gave the place a name
Two thousand shadowy, fateful years ago.

Here reared they walls and stately dwellings ; here
To gods Olympian builded many a shrine ;
Lived, loved and worshipped calmly by the clear
And beauteous inland ocean's azure brine.

Life held its sweets for them as now for us ;—
One great unswerving law controlleth all.
They changed glad songs and triumphs glorious
For solemn chant and gloomy funeral pall.

Thus did they pass,—and others came and passed ;
Fierce rapine languished, then fell grim decay,
Till all the splendor had been overcast
Save the grand temples standing here to-day.

Despoiled their altars, ravaged are their shrines,
  The lizard and the snake alone glide by ;
Yet nobly mute they face the Apennines,
  And still the old Greek grandeur typify.

In their Ionic majesty one finds
  The truest tokens that the past can show,—
What aspirations high moved mortal minds
  Two thousand shadowy, fateful years ago.

THE SENTINEL OF LUCERNE.

PILATUS, on thy rugged brow
  I watch the glancing sunlight play;
It brightens every pine-tree bough,
  And goldens all thy sombre gray.
Along thy lower slopes of green
  The gabled, red-roofed châlets stand,
Where thou, majestic in thy mien,
  Art monarch of this mountain land.

In placid breadth of glory lies
  Lucerne beneath thy beetling height
As sapphire as the clear June skies
  That arch above it, broad and bright.
And when no shrouding mist-wreath veils
  Thy kingly peaks, thou see'st below,
Like birds, fleet boats with snowy sails
  Across the dimpling waters go.

O thou that lookest down in scorn
  On lesser mounts that round thee gleam,
To me thou seem'st this perfect morn
  Like hallowed heights of which we dream ;
Where, in the shadowy days of eld,
  Those holy men, the prophets, trod,
And in the awesome silence held
  Communion with the voice of God.

THE MONK OF RAPPERSCHWYL.

WE climbed the hill at Rapperschwyl,
Up the steep steps of time-worn stone,
And rested where, in clouded air,
The castle, towered and turreted,
With clinging ivy overgrown,
Looked on the town beneath it spread,
And on the lake by breezes blown.

In hooded gown of russet brown
A monk with grizzled beard passed by
And those who played beneath the shade
Of leafy boughs that trembled near,
With clap of palms and merry cry
And childish laughter, low and clear,
Around him flocked as he drew nigh.

We saw the bright and genial light
  In eyes of more than worldly ken ;
We saw, the while, a kindly smile
    That wavered round his bearded mouth,
  With such swift radiance, as when
    A sunbeam glimmers from the south,
  And suddenly is gone again.

He paused to greet the faces sweet
  Upraised to his with eagerness ;
And as a bird above was heard
    In gush of song, he softly laid
  On shock and curl and braided tress
    Of happy boy and mirthful maid,
  His blameless hands as though to bless.

And we who viewed the merry brood,
  And marked the old monk's tender mien
Felt something in our breasts akin
    To broader sympathies uprise
  His simple act, his brow serene

Drove gloom from out the leaden skies,
And brightened all the sombre scene.

As down the hill at Rapperschwyl
Where frowned the castle, quaint and gray,
In hushed content we slowly went
While dreamily the day declined,
We bore no transient good away,
But high and holy thoughts enshrined
With the sweet memory of the day.

THE SWORD.

LIST to the song of a sword that hangs on high in the hall [wall
Of a bastioned border castle that bristles its great gray
Where a turbulent mountain stream leaps down with a madly-iterant brawl.

Long and bright is the brand, and it shines as it shone of old
When a ray through the western oriel strikes athwart its inlaid gold;
And a single diamond lustres keen below where the hand laid hold.

They tell of a magical forge where the glistering blade was wrought;
That a wizard tipped its point to pierce with the sting of a venomed thought;
And how the knight who flashed it first with the swarthy Paynim fought.

They tell of the oath he swore on the Hill of Calvary,
Ere he homeward turned his bronzèd face o'er the long
waste leagues of sea,
That none should bear that sacred steel unless for the
Christ it be.

Many the hands, 'tis said, that brandished it broad afar;
And ever it glowed in the battle's front as the conflict's
splendent star; [bar.
As mighty to turn the onset's tide as the swift Excali-

But there came a morn when one rode out 'gainst a
Christian foe,
And they bore him home at the day's dark death by
the awful sword laid low;
An arm unseen had poised the blade in its deep, heart-
cleaving blow.

And never again was it borne to the fight,—no, never
again;
For naught could purge from its tarnished tip the mark
of the sanguine stain; [slain.
And still a fear withholds the hand lest another soul be

Such is the song of the sword that hangs on high in the hall
Of a bastioned border castle that bristles its great gray wall
Where a turbulent mountain stream leaps down with a madly-iterant brawl.

IN ENGLAND.

To-morrow for the States,—for me
England and yesterday.

ROBERT LOUIS STEVENSON.

O WIELDER of the wizard pen,
Your loyal love I read
For highland moor and lowland fen,
For Thamis and for Tweed.

Your floods and fields are fair to see;
Here is your home and hearth.
And true your great heart could but be
To what is *mother earth.*

As you felt there an alien, I
An alien here must feel;
Though kindly is the English sky
And English friends are leal.

Yours is the love-glow in the breast
  For England's lakes and leas,
But mine for our "morn-mounting" West
  Beyond the wide wild seas.

A YACHTING SONG.

KEEN is the clear free air,
Sharp with a salty tang
Far o'er the waters blown,
Blown on the winds that fly ;
Up with the topsail there !
Gray have the shore-lines grown,
Dim where the mountains sprang
Bold, as we turned toward Skye.

Never a flaw in the breeze,
A fair and favoring gale,
Never a guy-rope wrong,
Never a sheet awry !
Over the summer seas,
Gay as a lover's song,
Merrily on we sail
Up to the straits of Skye.

There is the land at last,
Looming aloft afar ;
Nearer and still more near,
See how the shore slips by !
Inlet and point are past ;
Friends, we will harbor here.
Meadow and slope and scar,—
Cheer for the isle of Skye !

Let them prate of their joy,
Footing firm on the earth,
O they may prate who will,
Ours is the joy, say I !
Bliss of the buoyant boy,
Tremble and throb and thrill,—
Sound of the wild sea's mirth
Loud on the strand of Skye.

GHOSTS.

OVER a sea that shone like glass
Softly we sailed away,
And the white clouds lay in a heavy mass
On the breast of rising day.

We saw loom out of the mist
Hills that were vaguely high,
That faded in gray and in amethyst
Into the morning sky.

They seemed so wierd and vast,
(Wraiths of an awful woe,)
They are ghosts, we thought, of the lands of the past
That the sea gulfed long ago.

IN THE CATHEDRAL AT COLOGNE.

THE morning light in ever-growing glory
Sifts through the wondrous windows brightly down,
And clothes the saints of sacred life and story
Each with a lustrous golden robe and crown.

It streams o'er shadowy aisles ; on stately column
It plays with shifting gleams ; it pierces where
In shrinèd nooks, with faces worn and solemn,
Poor penitents are lifting hands in prayer.

There is no sound of song or organ swelling,
No low intoning, and no censer swayed ;
And yet the silence in that temple dwelling
Seems grander than the noblest anthem played.

Each arch is eloquent with holy meaning ;
  A sermon breathes from every carven scroll ;
Each senseless block becomes a field for gleaning
  Some seed of truth worth sowing in the soul.

Here, with the glorious rays of sunlight pouring
  O'er all in fulgent floods of heavenly birth,
Like some swift bird far into ether soaring,
  The heart transcends the grosser things of earth.

FROM HELOUAN.

WHEN day had run its sultry span,
 And shadows long the camels traced,
I saw the sun from Helouan
 Sink red behind the Libyan waste.

One *dahabeyeh* sail aslant
 Above the nearer palms rose high;
The pyramids, like adamant
 Triangles, cut the western sky.

The amethyst dusk veiled palm and pile
 And sail of Nubia-faring barge
And o'er the windings of the Nile
 The orient moon rose round and large.

Then, while its light lay on the land,
 I thought, as winds sighed like the lute,
Of Ramses prostrate in the sand,
 And Memnon's lips forever mute.

The past seemed like a scroll outspread ;
  I viewed it all, yet could not see,
Howe'er with unsealed eyes I read,
  Its wierd, oppressive mystery.

The low lute-tonèd south-wind fell ;
  I caught the desert's parching breath
O'er all lay vast, inscrutable,
  The calm solemnity of death.

A KAFFEYEH.

WHERE Tigris sees the orange bloom
'Twas wrought upon a Bagdad loom ;
Then some devout and pious hand
To Mecca bore it o'er the sand,
That it might catch the healing grace
Which breathes about the sacred place,
Beholding mosque and minaret
Above Mohammed's birthplace set.

Thence was it borne, and dearly sold
For discs of dull Egyptian gold.
In Nile-laved Cairo did it stay
Until one fair mid-winter day,
When its bright colors chanced to please
A Christian, wandering over seas,
Who brought it back with him ; and now
It feels the snow of Paula's brow,

Or by cool western winds is blown
When round her shapely shoulders thrown.

And unto her by it is lent
The glamour of the Orient;
Till every time I mark her stir
I think of attared rose and myrrh,
Or sapphire-cinctured skies that dream
O'er dusky Egypt's sacred stream;
And in her eyes I seem to see
An East that shines for none but me.

MOONLIGHT IN THE ORIENT.

THE moon we see through palm-trees shine,
  Is it the selfsame moon they know
Where now beyond the angry brine
  New England's hills are white with snow?
  Benignly evening's breezes blow,
Bats blunder blackly by, but there
  Keen winds go blaring to and fro,
And few may breast the baffling air.

We heard the clear muezzin-call
  Float from a distant airy height,
Where, with its lines of tapering wall,
  A minaret ascends the night;
  Now in the flood of falling light
Those silent summits seem to sway;
  Will they not vanish from the sight
Ere dawns another arid day?

Ah ! no ; albeit the crescent now
  Bears not the glory that it knew
When over Saladin's swart brow
  El Islam's conquering banners flew ;
  Not yet the cross may rule the blue
That spans the sand-swept Memphian plain,
  And many moons will wax anew
Before there comes the final wane

Yet it will come. That lucent arc,
  Swung far in sapphire air, shall see
Its counterpart grow dim and dark,
  Lost in the broad futurity.
  But no less fair its beams will be
Here in the summer's endless glow,
  Or where, ere winter's legions flee,
New England's hills are white with snow.

ASCALON.

UPON the semi-spherèd town
We from its ruined walls looked down;
Beyond us whitened leagues of sea,
Around us glowed anemone
And golden bloom and blossoms wan
At Ascalon.

Great wind-borne drifts of sand lay deep
On highways sunk in centuried sleep ;
And where the sand ceased, over all
Thick brambles lorded, rankly tall,
While dazzlingly the sunlight shone
O'er Ascalon.

It was a peaceful scene, but we
Recalled, and nowise dreamily,
The day when Richard Lion-heart
Here played his valiant-handed part,
And led the battle on and on
At Ascalon.

We saw the crescent and the cross
Above the surging squadrons toss ;
The swords and scimetars flash bright
Round helm and turban met in fight.
Where are they now ?—All, all are gone
From Ascalon !

Unless, perchance, when clear around
The moon illumes each brambled mound,
They marshall forth and charge again,
Those warriors in a ghostly train,
And struggle till the verging dawn
At Ascalon

Howe'er this be, by day-time all
Is calm about the gateless wall ;
Soon nature too will sink in sleep
Before the sand's annulling sweep.
A name,—no more will linger on
Of Ascalon.

THE GROTTO OF PAN.

NEAR where marshy Merom lies
Jordan has its crystal rise ;
From a grot's deep heart it springs
With eternal murmurings.
Pampas grass is feathery tall
Where it falls with rhythmic fall ;
Tiny poplars silver nigh
Where it dimples coolly by ;
Constant summer never flees,—
'Tis the haunt of bird and breeze ;
Fruit and flower in endless round
Render it enchanted ground.
Compassed soft by rainbow hues,
Fed by Hermon's generous dews,
Frowned upon by mountains bare,
Fair it seems, forever fair.

Long ago the Romans came,
Gave the spot a sacred name,
Hearing melody conveyed
In the sound the waters made
Such as oft they'd heard before
On the Anio's olived shore ;
Deeming it was Pan whose tongue
On the air such music flung.
Here, anear the mountain's base,
In the scarred cliff's lichened face,
Cut they shrines you still may see
To the goat-hoof deity.
Here at morning would they bring
Some pure flower-thank-offering ;
Here at evening would they lay
Reeds whereon the god might play.

Heaped above their bones behold
Centuries of dust and mould
Unto him they held divine
Now is reared no marble shrine.

Truth has been revealed to us ;—
Life seems more felicitous.
Yet sometimes we backward set
Faces shadowed by regret,
Mourning that shag-bearded Pan
Never fluted, never ran
Through the bloomy dingle sweet
With swift lift of cloven feet.
And the pagan in us still
Leaps to life with buoyant will,
And we cry with joyous cry,
Dreaming the lost god slips by.

BAALBEC.

WITH wasting day the violent tempest dies,
And slowly all the dense-banked clouds that hang
Above the high horizon's mountain line
Throw off their gloomy hues ; the hidden sun
With lavish alchemy inweaves a web
Of delicate damask and of glowing gold
And casts upon them. Hoary Lebanon,
With its unbosomed snow, grows palely rose,
And those majestic temples, where the gods
Of antique days had sacrificial shrines,
Bulk their maimed walls and columns grandly vast
Against the sovereign glory of the west.

Had such a sunset happed in olden time,
How all the sacred city's prosperous folk
Forth would have flocked, and ta'en the holy way
That led them templeward, and while the light

Dimmed o'er the virgin whiteness of stern peaks,
Have bowed themselves in worship! How the priests,
Setting calm faces toward the sinking orb,
Throwing sweet spices on undying fires,
Would have upraised their chant!

Now swallows swerve
In twittering flight above marred architraves,
Slim poplars whiten, and young mulberries
Give silken promise. In the squalid streets
Where slothful Arabs doze in dirt-walled shade,
The lean curs snarl, or sleep, or snap at flies.
Swift comes the dusk, prophetic of the stars,
And then the stars with their inviolate arc
Of peaceful beams, and Night o'er Baalbec
Draws her enfolding silence like a veil

PRINCESS BADOURA.

NIGHT is regent of the sky ;
All is still in Ispahan.
On the veined pomegranate-leaves
That the fragrant breezes fan
Floods of silver moonlight lie ;
Plaintively the bulbul grieves,
And the tinkling fountains flow
In the garden-close below ;
She, above on her divan
By the casement's open bars,
Gazes out upon the stars,
Happy Princess Badoura.

To the slave girl standing near
Wistfully and low she speaks,
Looking still into the night ;
Persian roses dye her cheeks,
And against her olive ear
Shines a pure pearl, snowy white.

Round her, like a filmy veil,
Falls her burnoose, azure pale ;
And a gleaming golden spear,
Like a ray of sunlight fair,
Shimmers in her raven hair,
    Lovely Princess Badoura.

At her feet there falls a rose ;
'Tis the longed-for trysting-hour !
Stooping with an eager air
Tenderly she clasps the flower,
Kisses it the while she goes
Swiftly down the winding stair ;
There her exiled lover waits
Till he sees the postern gates
Slowly, silently unclose,
And before him stand, divine
In the moonlight hyaline,
    Smiling Princess Badoura.

Oh, the joy that fills her heart
Once again to hear his voice,
Once again to feel his kiss !

All the birds that see rejoice,
Singing with melodious art,
"Ne'er before was love like this!"
What is now the world to her—
Noble, princely flatterer,
Playing each his petty part?
Here beneath the gemmèd skies,
Here is bliss and paradise!
Trustful Princess Badoura.

Hearken! on her startled ear
Falls a low and boding sound;
Is it but the winds that blow?
Is it but the kennelled hound?
Through her bosom thrills a fear
As the silent moments go.
Suddenly a scimetar
Flashes like a falling star,
And upon the grassy ground,—
With the love-light in his eyes
Fading fast,—her lover lies,
Woeful Princess Badoura.

A BIT OF MARBLE.

THIS bit of polished marble—this—
Was found where Athens proudly rears
Its temple-crowned Acropolis
So hoar with years.

In antique time some sculptor's hand,
Deft-turning, carved it fine and small,
A part of base, or column grand,
Or capital.

Pentelicus' white heart it knew
Before the chisel fashioned it ;
Long ere so fair of form it grew,
And delicate.

Regarding it, I mind me so
A song should be, with ardor wrought,—
Cut in the firm Pentelic snow
Of lofty thought.

FROM PENTELICUS.

THE wind came blaring up the mountain gorges ;
We heard it where we stood,
Like mad bacchantes at their frantic orgies
Within some lonely wood.

From a grim cairn we northward set our faces ;
Below us, far away
Stretched Marathon's wide plain with grain-sown spaces,
And its blue sickle bay.

How in our hearts, beholding it before us,
Did olden memories rise
Of those brave Greeks who charged with full-voiced chorus
Of Attic battle cries ;

Of Persian hosts in wildering disorder,
And mangled heaps of slain,
Of crimson stains that made a ghastly border
To fields of trampled grain !

And then there passed before our eyes the vision
Of that swift youth who fled
To Athens at the conflict's stern decision,
Gasped " victory," and fell dead.

Olympus, proud, pyramidal and peerless,
Clear in the distance rose ;—
We felt that he, the sacrificial, fearless,
Had kissed its deathless snows.

THE MÆNADS.

FROM the woodland gnarled and gray,
Where the leafage dims the day,
With a clash of cymbals loud,
Through the grasses, zephyr-bowed,
Where the slumberous poppies burn,
Raising each a fiery urn,
Comes a throng with frantic air,
Following fast a fleeing hare.

Wild the gleam that lights their eyes,
Strange the clamor of their cries ;
Ivy binds their glistening brows,
Twined with sprays from myrtle boughs.
Each a slender spear upholds ;
Leopard skins, in tawny folds,
Partly hide and partly show
Limbs as white as winter snow.

One restrains with leathern rein
Sinewy, sleek-limbed panthers twain ;
One waves high, with motions lithe,
Mottled snakes that hiss and writhe ;
And another bears along
Wine to cheer the masking throng,
Brewed by Bacchus in a still
High upon Hymettus hill.

Woe to him who meets this band
Faring through the forest land !
Earth shall know his face no more ;
Like that hapless youth of yore
In the sweet Arcadian days,
Deep in sunless beechen ways
Lifeless he shall lie, and cold,
Trampled out of mortal mould.

ORPHEUS.

I.

FARING forth and forward fleetly,
 Shepherd, o'er the daisied wold,
Piping long and piping sweetly
 On the reed your fingers hold,
Many an echoing answer will you
Hear from off the hills to still you,
Hear to rapture and to thrill you,
 Straying from your wattled fold.
Rustling leaves will calm to listen,
 Shrilling winds will hush to hear,
Startled eyes will turn and glisten
 Of the thicket-thridding deer.

Well-a-day!
Seek—in vain your sure divining!
Mourn—in vain your tearful pining!
Orpheus will flee away.

II.

None have played whose fingers fleeter
O'er the mellow pan-pipes ran,
None have lyred a music sweeter
Than his airs Æolian.
Though they haunt us from the May-time
Through the fragrant hours of hay-time
At the purple marge of daytime,
Grasp the strains we never can.
Follow, ever footing faster,
Yet the cadence still eludes ;
Both are wraiths, the reed and master,
From the Stygian solitudes.

Well-a-day !
Seek—in vain your empty calling !
Mourn—in vain your tear drops falling !
Orpheus will flee away.

THE CRUCIFIX.

YOU know Siena?—how fair a crown
On the fruitful Tuscan hills she shines?
How her streets go clambering up and down,
And how her walls, that are topped by towers,
Look out over slopes of verdant vines
And lemon groves and mulberry bowers
And olive orchards billowing far
To where the crests of the Apennines
Proud and purple and lordly are?
The glamour and glory of olden years
Is the royal robe that enfolds her now;
Like a mourning maiden with clouded brow
She grieves and grieves, yet she has no tears
For her splendors dead, but she silent waits
While the peasants plod through her unbarred gates,
Waits in her sadness and matchless pride
For a time to come, for a day new-born,

When her state shall again be glorified
By the magical gold of a risen morn.

The flooding amber of autumn-time
On the Tuscan hills lay rich and bright,
As I passed through the gate where all may see,
"Siena opens her heart to thee ;"
And the sound of a mellow noon-day chime
Was borne from a steeple's slender height.
Calm was the scene as I strode along
Up the winding *via*, and dreamy-eyed
Were the folk who loitered by, as though
Life lapsed for them like a slumberous song,
Or a peaceful river's placid tide
That quickens not in its seaward flow.
The great white oxen with large wide eyes
Looked upon me in wondering wise,
They seemed to know as I past them sped
That mine was an alien's rapid tread.
I had left the present far behind,
A languor lurked in the brooding air ;
Spectral voices spoke from the wind,

And I could but fancy, as up and down
I strayed through the streets of the lonely town,
That ghostly presences everywhere
Peopled the silence, and went and came,—
Cavalier and portly dame,
Haughty belles and perfumed beaus,—
All the pageant and pomp the same
As when Siena held her state
With those in Italy proudly great,
Leal to her friends and harsh to her foes.

At last, such a whimsical guide was chance,
My steps were led through a narrow way
Where the frowning walls shut out the day ;
And pausing a moment, I cast a glance
Back at the great cathedral square,
And the campanile towering tall,
A marble miracle wrought of old,
Limned on the clear sky's blue and gold,
Stately, straight and symmetrical.
Then, as I turned from the spot to fare,
I saw in an antique window there,

'Mid bronze and steel of the ancient days,
(Casques and blades and bits of mail,)
A quaint scrolled silver crucifix hang ;
And while I stood with marvelling gaze
Bent on the holy symbol, one
Whose face was wrinkled and drawn and pale,
Out from a low dark doorway sprang ;
He bowed with the gleam of a kindly eye
And a smile that was good to look upon ;
"Would Signor enter, would Signor buy ?"

I stooped and followed ; he gently took,
With reverence grave and a sacred sign,
The crucifix off from its tiny hook.
Carven characters strange and fine
Hid in the scroll-work fair I saw ;
Mystical, beauteous, void of flaw,
The crucifix lay in my palm outheld,
A heritage rich from the times of eld,—
That had pressed sweet lips ice-cold in the clay,
That had called the light to dark eyes long dim,
That had heard soft prayers at the edge of day,

'Neath the olive's shade, by the fountain's rim,
Or high in a latticed chamber, hung
With tapestry that swayed and swung
In the wind that paused on its minstrel way
And a tuneful gust through the casement flung.

"Would Signor buy?" again did I hear
The questioning voice that was low yet clear;
The dark deep eyes were upraised to mine.
"Too much for a bauble? Ah, Signor, see!"
And he took the crucifix tenderly,
Held it before me, and lightly pressed
A finger slim on its gleaming crest;
Then out from the cross like a sudden line
Of jeweled light, leaped a slender blade,
About whose quivering tip there played
Such hues as the ravished sight sees shine
When a bow of promise flings its arc
From cloud to cloud as the tempest dies,
And a jubilant burst of song the lark
Once more unbreasts to the grateful skies.

The old man smiled in a calm, grave way
As in startled wonderment I outcried ;
"Would Signor care for a space to bide
And hear the story ?" I heard him say.
I answered eagerly ; then, straightway,
Two chairs he brought and a table small,
And delicate fragile glasses twain ;
And down from a cupboard high in the wall,
Dusty, and marred with scar and stain,
He drew a flagon crooked and tall ;
And while I hearkened as in a spell,
With his brightening eyes fixed fast on mine,
This is the tale I heard him tell
'Twixt sips of the golden Asti wine.

* * * * * * * *

In the days of feud, in the days of power,
In the days of Guelph and Ghibbeline,
When hate in the heart like an evil flower
Took root and flourished, and choked the green
Soft shoots of love in that garden fair,
No senator noble among all

Who met in the spacious council-hall
Had wiser words or a grander air
Than the Count Nerucci. The luckless fate
That had robbed "my lord" of his gentle wife,
Had given the light of his lonely life,
A beautiful daughter, sweet and good,
Who had bloomed into peerless womanhood.

Stern with others, the Count for her
Had naught but kindness, and speech that hung
Soft word-caresses upon his tongue.
And never a wooing worshipper,
(Though many ardent and fond there were,)
Of those who sued for her hand and heart,
With much of feeling but more of art,
Was half so lover-like as he.
Perchance on the living one he tried
To shower more love, in the memory
Of his cold neglect of the one who died.
Bianca,—such was the name she bore,—
Was as skilled as the noblest maid of the time ;
She could win the lute to a tinkling chime,

Or thread the dance on the marble floor ;
Not one in all Siena than she
Had a defter hand for tapestry
She charmed each guest at her father's board
By her winsome loveliness and grace ;
A something breathed from her pure young face,
Looked from her eyes, shone from her brow,
Leaped from her lips as they shaped for a smile,
A fearless innocence free from wile
That made the veriest outcast bow ;
And every soul who had seen adored
Her beauty for many a Tuscan mile.

On all the youths who a-wooing came
Bianca smiled, but on each the same,
A frank sweet smile that seemed to say,
Ere a word of love had been spoken, "nay."
Yet had she dreams as all maidens do ;
But no one came with the form or voice
Of the valiant one she had dreamed her choice ;
And her father laughed as the number grew
Of those who would with his daughter wed.

"Thou lovest thy father," he ever said,
"Too well to fly to a suitor's arms."
So the calm days sped, and Bianca's charms
Drew ever more to her virgin shrine.

One fair springtime when the lusty vine
Along the valleys and up the hills
Its tender emerald had unfurled,
In the heart of the golden afternoon
Came Bianca forth from her bower ;
A bird with welcome of runs and trills
Above in a dizzying spiral whirled,
The buoyant breeze set the boughs in tune,
And the chaliced tulips flamed in flower.
The palace garden reached adown
A terraced slope to the massive wall
That girt the triple hills of the town.
Here to an arbor cool and small
Did the fair Bianca love to come,
And list to the fountain's drowsy fall,
A bird's low twittering, or the hum
Of the honey-sated bacchanal.

And here would she bring her silvery lute
To touch its strings were the garden mute,
And charm therefrom some jubilant strain
Lest the brooding silence seem like pain.
She swept the chords, and the music sweet
In fullest cadence throbbed and thrilled ;
And soon, from a neighboring green retreat,
To the strain with its ripple and rhythmic beat,
There rose a voice, and a glad love song
Was borne to her ear, till her heart was filled
With a strange great joy. Now soft, now strong,
Outrang the tones as her fingers ran
O'er the quivering strings, nor died away
Till in blushing marvel she ceased to play.
That night when the stars in a golden span
Athwart the sky threw their lucent gleams,
She heard that voice in her happy dreams.

Though the sweet Bianca knew too well
That beyond the wall, with its pleachèd green
Was the garden-close of a Florentine,
And though oft she had heard her father tell

How his hate of Florence ne'er would die,
Yet on the morrow she fain would go,
Ere the warm and westering sun sunk low,
And holding her lute in a trembling hand
Where the arbor screened from the peering sky,
Play the same clear strain she had played before,
And smile in joy when she heard once more
The pure strong voice and the buoyant song;
So day by day did the hours wax long
Till the one hour came when she might stand
In the shielding arbor's cool recess.
Soon the hope of a larger happiness
Had birth in her heart; and as first her ear
Had longed for the sound of that voice to rise,
So now did she cast her yearning eyes
Toward the barrier-wall, though half in fear.
At last one day at the wane of light,
When, loath to leave, she had lingered late,
With a sudden agile and airy bound
The singer vaulted the wall's gray height.
In fair Siena, or sister state,
Where'er might a wanderer chance to go,

Could no braver, handsomer youth be found
Than the minstrel-soldier Georgio.

They met as lovers ; they spoke as though
Their love was a thing that the years had known,
And not a flower that had burst and blown
Into instant bloom with its warmth and glow.
Fond and deep were the vows they breathed ;
And their new-learned names on each other's lips
Were ever with soft endearments wreathed
Till words in kisses had found eclipse.
And thus they parted, and thus they met
Each blissful day ere the sun had set.

So much did the maiden dwell alone,
Ruling the house as the moment willed,
So full was the mind of her father filled
With his statecraft schemes, that a month had flown
Since the first and fateful sunset hour
When the lovers met in the garden-bower.
Oft did Bianca's heart make moan
That the blameless Georgio was kin

To the father-hated race, that he
Was a soldier leal to the Medici,
In the eyes of her sire a most deadly sin.
She listened not when he would entreat
He might lay their cause at her father's feet,
But wavered ever 'twixt smile and sigh,
And swiftly thus did the days slip by.

Ah! those hours of love,—what a paradise
Each found in the other's brimming eyes!
Then a word, a smile, a look, a kiss,
Would fill their hearts with a perfect bliss.
How young they were, and how fondly they
Dreamed never a night would dim their day,
But all would fall by a kindly chance
Like the happy end of a fair romance,
And they would be wed ere the tiny fig
On the autumn boughs grew ripe and big,
Or lips by the juice of the grape were stained,
Or the red round moon of the harvest waned.

Alas, for the visions their eyes had known!—
One vesper-time when in tender tone

To the charmed Bianca Giorgio rea
A passionate love song of his own,
Without there sounded the rapid tread
Of nearing feet, and aside were thrown
The screening vines, and white with wrath,
Before the door in the narrow path
Stood the Count Nerucci. In vain they plead,—
In vain were the maiden's tears ; in vain
Did the eager lover strive to gain
From the ireful father a listening ear.
But the sire with a tense-strung voice and clear
To his daughter only spoke, and she,
Shrinking a moment, pale with fear
At his awful look, as the stricken flee
From a dreaded scourge or an evil ban,
Toward the palace doorway swiftly ran.
Then the Count turned fierce on the kneeling man
With a hissing vengeance-curse, and he,
Leaping back from the steel ere the stroke could fall,
Sprang out from the arbor and scaled the wall,
Lest his hand, uplifted in enmity,
Bring death and sorrow to whelm them all.

Never again did Bianca know
The bliss of love, or the overflow
Of joy and peace that her heart had known
In the calm sweet days that were fleet to go.
Shut from the world in her bower alone,
Her ceaseless longing became like pain.
The hours were links of an endless chain
That bound her closer and closer, till
It seemed to her that her throbbing brain
Would reel to frenzy. Her mind would fill
With vain wild thoughts of flight, and one
Went alway with her where'er she fled.
But keen eyes watched at the set of sun,
And keen eyes watched when the night was done,
And though never a warning word was said,
She grew to feel that the very wall
Hid hireling hands that would reach at call,
And drag her back, if she dared to tread
Beyond the bounds of the long dim hall
Where she walked at morn and at evenfall.

A loving father she knew no more;
He never smiled, and his visage wore

A dark, stern look as he daily came
And went, and she never heard her name
Slip through his lips as in time of yore.
And once when she prayed he would tell her when
She might be free in the air again,
He cried, as his face grew pale and set,
"When *he* is dead, and when you forget!"
And so, as a tender flower will fade
And waste away in the sterile shade
If neither the kindly sun nor shower
Prolong the span of its fragile hour,
She drooped, ere ever the reaper's blade
Had garnered the harvest's golden dower.

Tears for Siena. Her fairest lay
White and still in her marble bed;
Through chancel windows the full-orbed day
Flung rainbow beams ere the mass was said.
Mourn for Bianca. The rich and poor
Loved the maid who was sweet and pure;
And into the vast cathedral aisles
A throng of the high and the low had come,
And under the pillar's massive piles

They looked and listened with anguish dumb.
The solemn chanting fell and rose
In waves of sound to its mournful close;
Then the long procession formed, and passed
From the portals dim, and wended down
With a silent, measured step and slow,
And following blindly among the last,
His face half hid by his monk's black gown,
Was the grief-embittered Giorgio.

Erelong a gathering rumor ran
Through Siena streets that the Count was ill;
Remorse had broken the iron will,
And many a void day faint and wan
He lay at the very door of death;
But autumn came with its quickening breath,
And stirred the sluggish tide in his veins,
And a feeble flush on his pallid brow
Answered the flush on the woodland bough;
The air grew fresh with the healing rains,
Renewal that nature alone can give,
And 'twas noised abroad that the Count would live.

"Send for a priest," one morn he cried
To the serving-man by his couch's side;
"I have conquered death in this hateful strife,
And would give my thanks to the Lord for life!"
So a man went forth, and it happed near by
In a monk's long robe, and with downcast eye,
Walked one who seemed of a holy mien,
And who, when called, in a voice serene
Bade the servant lead, and with shaded face
Followed close behind at a rapid pace.
They passed the doorway and scaled the stair;
They threaded a corridor high and dim;
There were rustling sounds in the hangings there,
And the priest's white fingers long and slim
A silver crucifix clutched, as on
They hurried, till out of the haunted gloom
In swung the noiseless door of a room
Where the moted morning sunlight shone.
The monk, with his dark hood backward thrown,
Uplifted his face to the sudden glow,—
A young face saddened with lines of woe;
The servant turned, but he did not know

That the man he had left with the Count alone
Was the hated lover Giorgio.

Never again did they see that face
In camp or court or in festal place ;
When he went from the palace no one knew,
And whither, there never was found a clue.
But at Florence, in after time, 'twas told
How a monk who dwelt in a convent old
That on Vallombrosa's vale looks down,
Would sweetly sing in the cloisters brown
Sad songs through the tender twilight glow,
And his name was the Fra Biancino.

And the Count?—Long, long through the vaulted hall
Did the servants wait for his voice to fall ;
They hearkened in vain for a word or cry,
But they heard no sound as the hours dragged by.
So at last in fear did the bravest go
And tap at the door and listen in dread ;
A stir in the tapestry overhead
Made them tremble and quail and start ;
Then they sprang and opened the door, and lo !

On the sanguined couch the Count lay dead,
With a dagger-crucifix in his heart.

* * * * * * * *

The palsied hand of the man who told
This sad strange tale of the years of old,
Tipped the flagon and poured the wine ;
We quaffed; then he took the proffered gold
And the deadly crucifix was mine.
I sought the tortuous streets again,—
The square where the ancient palaces stand,
Looming desolate, dark and grand ;
Life was dead, and the grass upsprung
In the ways that hurrying feet once trod.
Black clouds had gathered in sombre train,
The thunder menaced with angry tongue,
And the lightning brandished its livid rod.
All Siena seemed to mourn ;
The trees by passionate sobs were torn ;
A sound of wailing came from the wind,
And I could but think of the long ago,—
Of fair Bianca the maid who pined,
And the minstrel-soldier Giorgio.

A TWILIGHT PIECE.

I STRAYED from the bower of the roses as the
  dusk of the day drew on,
From the purple palm-tree closes where the crimson
  cactus shone ;
Along the sycamore alley and up through the town I
  strode,
Nor paused where the gay groups dally at curves of the
  wide white road.
And I came to a pathway climbing through an olive
  orchard gray,
As the last faint bells were chiming in a chapel far
  away.
Only the stir of the lizard in the long sparse grass I
  heard,
And the wind, like an unseen wizard, with its mystical
  whispered word.

But at last I broke from the glooming of boughs, and
the darkling place,
And beheld tall warders looming o'er a wide and lonely
space ;—
Old cypress trees intoning a chant that was wierd and
low,
And as sad as the ghostly moaning from the lips of
the Long-ago.
Here many a time at the margin of day, ere the bats
grew brave,
Had I seen the low sun sink large in the dip of the
western wave ;
Seen the hues of the magical painter flush half of the
sky's broad zone,
And then grow fainter and fainter till the flowers of the
night were blown.
Enwrapt by the drowsy quiet, I sank on the turf, and
long
I yearned for the rhythmic riot of the night-bird's soar-
ing song ;
A song that should pulse and thrill me, and tides of
the heart unbar,

A song that should surge and fill me with thoughts of
a clime afar;
For I felt the passionate sadness of the mourner who
may not weep,
And turned to the bird's wild gladness as the weary
turn toward sleep.
Then it came, ah! it came with a rushing and ripple
of notes that poured
Like a mountain rillet gushing from a rock-fount,
pebble-floored ;
And I soared with the song's swift soaring, and I fled
with the song's swift flow,
From that land of the sun's adoring to a land of
storm and snow ;
From the home of the rose and laurel, from the olive
slopes and the vines,
To hills where the mad winds quarrel in the supple tops
of pines.
And I said, "enough of the languor, enough of the
dreamful ease,
With never a sound of anger from the slumberous
sapphire seas !

Give me the din of the battle of turbulent life once more,—
The clangor, the stress, the rattle, on the new world's strenuous shore ;
The hearts I love and that love me, and the frank, free, trustful eyes,
And the blue of the skies above me, the blue of my own dear skies! "
A moment the strains waxed stronger, then died ;—no, it might not be ;
I knew I must linger longer by the strange sweet southern sea ;
Linger and con from the stories of those who had left life's ways,
Linger and glean from the glories of the hallowed and haloed days.
But a moment more I tarried till the sovran moon rose up,
And the land and the heaven were married by the wine from its gold-bright cup ;
Then I swiftly downward wended, and was glad once more to be

Where the laughter clear ascended by the shore of the siren sea.
Ah! the lone heart, backward turning, though fair be the skies that dome,
Must sometimes feel a yearning for the happy hills of home.

THE SEASONS ROUND.

CARMEN HIEMIS.

A TYRANT rules the land !
With icy hordes invincible he came,
From far boreal realms that bear no name,
And on our fields let loose his ravening band.
In vain the struggle 'gainst such frenzied foes ;
Before the imperious onset of the snows,
Our sovereign's army fled in wild dismay.
Now, looking forth, we see,—
Reft of their robes and royal livery,—
Long captive lines in dismal disarray.

Through night and day above the tapering firs,
The cruel monarch's blatant trumpeters
Their shrill *reveillés* blow ;
Leaps the sharp sound
Up the wide arch to heights without a bound,
Along the hills and through the vales below.

Where'er the eye
May sweep beneath the cloud-embattled sky,
In vestiture immaculate the meadows lie.
Earth's leaping crystal veins,
That furrowed far the harvest-goldened plains
While leafy banners tossed,
Are manacled by pallid-fingered Frost.
And we who trod
Not long aforetime on the yielding sod
Of woodland slopes that gleamed with golden-rod,
Draining large life from multitudinous things,—
The lymph of flower-lipped springs,
The lithe vines' spiralings,—
Now gather round the friendly-flaming fire,
As the slow hours expire.

And yet, if joy be with us, what care we
For all of Winter's ruthless savagery,
Forgetful not, the while
The maskèd heavens glimpse no flashing smile,
Of a whole-souled, wide-handed charity!
Have we not song for cheer,

And tune-enchanted strings to trance the ear?
And may we not retreat
To some deep window-seat,
And hold communion, through clear-lettered page,
With hallowed saint and sage
Of high-browed Learning's every age?
May we not glide
Down the melodious tide
Wherefrom of old there sprung
Celestial Poesy of the silver tongue,
And, though the low skies frown, forever find
Unnumbered Italys in the cloudless mind?

Ah! well we know
This riotous ruler that we hold our foe,
Erelong, in impotence of swift overthrow,
Will northward lead his horde
Along the stern sea-board
To wan demesnes of frozen field and floe.
With what a generous hand
The conqueror will lavish on the land
The emerald largess of his empery

That fronts the surges of the Southern sea !
The charmèd winds will bear their fragrant freight ;
The rills, rejuvenate,
Will voice the grateful gladness of the earth ;
And everywhere,
Throughout the halcyon spaces of clear air,
Will choral harmonies have joyful birth.

Will not this zone of music be to us
A guerdon bounteous
For all the silent grayness of dead hours ?
Then mourn thou not, for soon, faint-hearted one,
Through the soft pattering of mild vernal showers
Will gleam the gladdening sun,
And thou shalt know,
As if from far creation's source should roll,
The ecstasy of life's sweet overflow,
And a divine uplifting of the soul.

AN APRIL SONG.

PERCHED upon a maple bough,
Sang a wren, "'Tis April now!"
And the while he tuned his trills,
Leaped the rills,
Flushed the hills,
And a hint of coming glory gleamed upon the mountain's brow.

Down beside the reedy mere
Piped a blackbird, "April's here!"
And the water murmured low
In its flow,
"Soon will blow
Lovely golden-petaled lilies for the blushing maiden Year."

Sweetly from the woodland's heart
With his ever-joyous art,
"April's come," a robin cried;
"March has died;
Winds that sighed,
Mourning, moaning round the gables, play a merry lover's part."

On an elm-tree branch asway,
Caroled forth a joyous jay;
Clear from his exuberant throat
Note on note
Seemed to float,—
"Joy in sun and joy in shower,—April ushers in the May!"

A MAY CAROL.

MAY,—and the spray of the apple
  Glows in the orchard aisles;
May,—and the gay hues dapple
  Meads with their rolling miles.

Bright is the light downpouring,
  Clear is the heaven and calm;
High through the sky go soaring
  Birds from the land of balm.

Up from the cup of morning
  Redolent perfumes rise,
Where, with its fair adorning,
  Dewv the garden lies.

Sweet is the beat of singing
  Brooks in their seaward flight;
Far is the starlight flinging
  Gleams through the hush of night.

Bud,—and the blood is hastened ;
  Bloom,—and the heart grows gay ;
Leaf,—and the grief that chastened
  Dies at the dawn of May.

A JUNE HARMONY.

A BIRD in the boughs sang "June,"
And "June," hummed a bee
In a bacchic glee
As he tumbled over and over,
Drunk with the honey-dew ;
Then the woods took up the tune
And the rippling runnels too,
The tune of the bird that sang in the tree
And the bee that buzzed in the clover.

And "June," cried the leaves in time,
Till crickets at night
With a wild delight
Sang "June" to the moon downbeaming,
"June" to the moon and stars;

And the grasses seemed to chime
With the music's mellow bars,
While butterflies danced with airy flight
In the sunlight amber-gleaming.

And the flowers were glad that swayed
In the breeze whose tune
Was forever "June";
The rose and the regal lily,
The humble blooms of the mead,
The fragile ferns in the glade,
The quivering rush and reed,
All joyed in the azure afternoon
And the morn and the evening stilly.

And the song in every heart
Found echo, and rang
While the green hills sang
With a throb and thrill of pleasure;
Alike the old and the young,

As they felt their pulses start,
To their musical mirth gave tongue,
Till from vale and hill the chorus sprang
In a swelling, merrying measure.

O joy to be out in June
'Neath the cloudless blue
In the dawn and dew
'Mid the ruddy buds of clover,
To be out, alert and free !
For life is a precious boon
With the world in harmony,
When June wakes love in the heart anew,
And the cup of bliss brims over.

A MIDSUMMER HARBINGER.

WHAT time, this very morn,
Untiring chanticleer had loudly blown
Twice, or yet thrice, his wakening matin horn,
Arousing, did I hear
A sharp, continuous, lone,
Persistent rasping, as of tense-drawn strings
A moment grating on my sleep-dulled ear ;
Then did it seem to grow
To sound of doubtful cadence, quavering low,
And die away in broken murmurings.

Herald of heated hours,
Shrill harbinger of lifeless breezes borne
From lands where bloom the heavy-chaliced flowers,
We gladly bid thee hail ;
For June's wind-scattered buds we will not mourn.

What though the rose is withered at the core, [fail,
 What though the limpid fountains thirst and
 What though, in heaven's mid-height,
 The dog-star burns its lambent fires by night,
And the clear vernal songs are heard no more!

The poppy flames for us;
 On daylight's verge the full-toned whippoorwill
Makes purple twilight-time harmonious.
 The fruit boughs ruddier grow;
 The yawning granary mows that are to fill
Gladden with rich increase from harvesting;
 Our hearts have joy in summer's overflow,
 For though seed-time be fair,
 Diviner far unto the hands that share
The affluent season of the garnering.

AS AUGUST COMES.

IN dull monotony of heat
  The hazy hills and lowlands lie,
And billow till they blend and meet
  With lurid amplitudes of sky.

The locust's shrilly fife-note cleaves
  The fervid air, a knife of sound,
As August comes with poppy leaves
  Around his swarthy temples bound.

AS WANES THE YEAR IN AUTUMN-TIDE.

AS wanes the year in Autumn-tide,
With flaunting pageantry and pride,
The bannered woodlands far unfold
Their bounty of ungathered gold.
The milkweed sends its silken sails
Adown the tide of gentle gales,
Presaging snow-flakes that will fall
When skies o'erlean,—a dull gray wall,
And frail leaf-shallops wander wide,
As wanes the year in Autumn-tide.

The hue that gleams upon the vine
Foretells the sparkle of the wine ;
The sumach's beacon, crimson-bright,
Doth harbinger the hearthstone's light ;
The weaver-spiders deftly fling

Their looms on boughs that sough and swing ;
There is a sound of singing flight
From noon of day till noon of night ;
And hours like rainbowed bubbles glide,
As wanes the year in Autumn-tide.

Re-nascent with tne winds that came
And touched the crocus into flame,
Supreme through Summer's splendid day,
Now Nature ripens to decay ;
And yet, within my heart I find
No vain desires, no longings blind ;
With steadfastness I turn my eyes
To what in Winter darkness lies ;
And harboring hope, the days I bide,
As wanes the year in Autumn-tide.

IN LATE NOVEMBER.

I WALKED afield one morn in late November,
The sun was hidden and the air was chill ;
And not a sumach showed a glowing ember
Along the windy summit of the hill ;
No lordly linden showered its gold above the swollen rill.

I listened long to catch a bird-note falling
From out the sombre spaces of the sky,
And only heard a grim rook hoarsely calling
As toward the woodland he went wheeling by ;
The sere marsh rushes seemed to breathe an echo to my sigh.

When last I strayed this self-same pathway over
How every breeze was palpitant with song !
The grass I trod was white with foamy clover,
And bees went darting by, a burdened throng ;
Now all was drear and desolate the whole wide vale along.

Where is the promise of the re-awaking ?
  I thought, as one that o'er dead joyance grieves,
Some lingering springtide symbol sweetly making
  A link between the reaped and unsown sheaves ;
  When lo, a violet still in bloom amid the withered
      leaves !

BESIDE THE INGLE

WE who by the genial fire
Watch the windy hours expire,
Hearing down the chimney whine
Blasts that toss the stanchest pine,
Seeing wan and dreary lie
Barren fields beneath the sky,
Such a guerdon have that we
Care not what without may be.

That an icy spell is flung
O'er the rillet's tuneful tongue;
That the snows engird and fret
Banks where bloomed the violet;
That no leaf may front the sun
Save the wizened ghost of one,
All,—like visions fade and flee
From the paths of memory.

Song has made the ingle fair ;
Song has warmed the wintry air ;—
Shakespeare's well-spring, draught divine,
Milton's deep, sonorous line,
Scott's pure fountain welling up,
Keats to brim the wondrous cup ;—
All the drops since time began
Of the dews Parnassian !

SONNETS AND QUATRAINS.

FROM THE CASTLE TERRACE.

(*Heidelberg.*)

WHERE courtly knights and maidens long ago,
In the soft light of fading afternoon,
Heard the sweet cadence of some minstrel's tune
Float up the walls from garden-paths below,
We sit to-day and watch the dying glow
Of sunrays bright on summer lands aswoon,
And hold the silence as a golden boon,
And do not heed how gliding moments flow.

The Neckar winds from out the wooded hills,
Silvers the valley, laves the quaint town's quays,
And wanders westward in a gleaming line ;
Far-following the sinuous path it fills,
Through undulating, unreaped harvest-seas,
Upon our vision dawns the storied Rhine.

PARIS REVISITED.

AGAIN the pleasure-seeking throng I see,
Again a voyager on the buoyant tide,
Adown the brilliant boulevards I glide
Where all is light and mirth and vanity.
Laughter upleaps as does a bird set free,
Darts down the air and sounds on every side ;
The Present is the godhead glorified,
And small the holden heed of time to be.

Strife seems a stranger here. The air breathes balm ;
Unclouded, domes the sky in peaceful blue
O'er pleasure's night-increasing carnival ;
And yet one tragic touch would change it all,
Would kindle passion's baleful fires anew,
And show the tiger sleeping 'neath the calm.

THE FIRST SIGHT OF ROME.

I SAW across the wide Campagna rise
The dome that crowns St. Peters, and I knew
At last were eager, youthful dreams come true,
And bright above me beamed the Roman skies.
There flowed the Tiber, there before my eyes,
Eternal hill on hill in fair full view
The city lay, and as I nearer drew,
"Roma! Roma!"—I heard the olden cries.

How through my brain, when, clashing on my ear,
These shrill shouts fell, scenes strangely stirring ran!
I saw triumphal columns marching home,
The Colosseum crowded, tier o'er tier,
The gladiatorial combat, man to man,
And all the splendor that once gloried Rome.

THE BAY OF NAPLES.

ERE yet I viewed thee, fair things had I said
Of thy expanse, O sapphire-shining bay ;
But having seen, alas ! what shall I say?
Marking thy beauty seems my cunning fled.
In purple shrouded, Capri lifts her head
Upon the pale horizon far away ;
And now that night is hand in hand with day
From grim Vesuvius' cone the cloud has fled.

That ominous disc of light above thee shows
Thou hast a shadow, darksome as is death,
Glooming above thy fairness evermore ;
And when it may, no lore-wise prophet knows,
With visitation of its fatal breath,
Lay desolate all thy lovely curve of shore.

A DAMASCUS PICTURE.

DIM day-wane at Damascus. White afar
Hermon uplifts a glistening crown of snow ;
In long ungainly lines the camels go
From weary windings of low-roofed bazar.
The brow of Anti-Lebanon stands a bar
Of gloomy black against the western glow ;
Cool Barada leaps by with restless flow,
And coming night reveals her first clear star.

Hark !—faintly from yon tapering minaret
Sounds the muezzin's oft-repeated call
That bids the turbaned faithful come to prayer;
Turn south toward Mecca. There, slim, slant-wise set,
And trembling to inevitable fall,
A palm-tree rears its withered bulk in air.

SUMMER NOON.

THE air is full of soothing sounds. The bee
Within the waxen lily's honeyed cells,
In monotone of mellow measure tells
His yet unsated joyance; drowsily
The swallows spill their liquid melody
As down the sky they drop, and faintly swells
The tremulous tinkle of the far sheep bells,
While wind-harps sigh in every crownèd tree.

Beneath the beechen shade the reapers lie,
Upon their lips a merry harvest tune;
Knee-deep within a neighboring stream, the kine
Stand blinking idly in the clear sunshine;
And like a dream of olden Arcady
Seems the sweet languor of the summer noon.

A PEARL.

ROUND as the roc's egg of the Arab tale,
And flawless white as was that fabled sphere,
I see it shine below my lady's ear,
This prize-plucked bauble from an ocean vale.
Was it where round Ceylon the swift ships sail,
A daring diver clove, without a fear,
Palm-shaded waves through fathoms emerald clear,
And brought it forth 'mid strenuous shout and hail?

Methinks from some far eastern isle it came,
Because it giveth to her tranquil face
An orient languor and a slumberous grace;
But where, O where, in lands without a name,
Near what soft cheek's pure-glowing altar flame
Could it have found so fair a resting place?

THE STATUE.

AS perfect in their symmetry as thine,
O inarticulate marble lips, were those
My love once raised to mine, yet tinged with rose
And freighted with a redolence divine.
Her poise of head was queenly; fair and fine
Her alabaster arms that shamed the snows;
Her gracious bearing had thy pure repose,
And stately was she as the forest pine.

Knowledge sat throned upon her regal brow,
Round which her tresses rippled, bright as gold;
Sweet as a songbird's on a budding bough
The liquid voice that from her lips outrolled;
But lo! there came an awful change, and now
Thou, in thine icy hush, art not more cold!

THE MENDICANT.

LIKE some way-weary mendicant came I
Unto the court where Love holds potent reign,
And there in desolation I was fain
Before the gateway to lie down and die.
But one came forth who heard my mournful cry,
Nor mocked nor spurned me with a cold disdain,
But cheered me, saying: "Do not nurse thy pain;
Be brave and bid the ghosts of dead days fly!"

Then I arose and cast the Past aside,
And felt within my breast a gladness great,
Meeting the glorious eyes that beamed above;
And all the future time was glorified,
For I, who was a beggar at the gate,
Became a dweller in the court of Love.

WHEAT.

BEHOLD a billowy sea of golden spears
  That to and fro in every breeze that blows
  Tosses its amber waves, and proudly shows
Bright scarlet poppies when the warm wind veers.
Hearken, and lo! there falls upon the ears
  A song as mellow as the one that rose
  From Boaz' fields at daytime's drowsy close
And thrilled his heart in those dim Hebrew years.

And the swart mower, leaning on his scythe
To catch the swelling music, clear and blithe,
  Thinks, as his eyes with love-light brim and glow,
That she who sings, the while the bright beams fade,
Is far diviner than the lovely maid
  Who gleaned in fields Judean long ago.

THE ACTOR.

Night after night a mimic death he died,
While sympathetic thousands wept and sighed;
But when at last he came in truth to die,
No teardrop fell from any mourner's eye.

MARBLE.

A blank unshapely mass but yesterday,
As void of beauty as a clod of clay;
Behold, a miracle!—for now it seems
A form to haunt the midnight of our dreams.

ICICLES.

These are the weapons that the sword-smith, Cold,
Has forged to make the ranks of Winter bold;
But when the Sun his shimmering lances throws,
How are they shivered by the silent blows!

MILKWEED.

We see upon this wild November air
  White, downy couriers wing their eager way ;
Upon what hasty errandry they fare,
  And whither, who can say ?

DIAMONDS.

About her neck they gleam in lustre bright,
Like stars that glisten on the zone of Night :
Yet more than Afric's flawless gems I prize
Soft Pity's jewels in her loving eyes.

HOME SONGS.

THE ROCKY MOUNTAINS.

THERE is a land where effluent sunshine falls
On the white splendor of sheer mountain walls,
From whose pale peaks and many-caverned passes
The hollow voice of iterant echo calls.

Aloft it towers above the pathless plains ;
Within its bounds grim desolation reigns,
Save where upspring the hardy flowers and grasses
In narrow clefts when wrathful winter wanes.

Eternal snows upon its bosom lie ;
It holds communion with the unfathomed sky
Through circling years of unrecorded changes,
While mighty nations spring to life, and die.

Beneath its crags uplifting, dome on dome,
The everlasting glaciers have their home ;
The storm-undaunted eagle boldly ranges
Round loftiest peaks by human feet unclomb.

It has for warders ranks of regal pines
That skirt its borders in majestic lines,
    Their lances ever in the keen air tossing
At earliest morn, or when the day declines.

Impetuous streams are born, where, winding miles
Deep in its dark and dangerous defiles,
    No gleaming rays of golden sunlight crossing,
Brighten the dim, sepulchral, rocky aisles.

Nature reveals her deepest, grandest moods
Within its vast unpeopled solitudes;
    And when the purple night's gray mists are drifting,
A sense of the Divine above it broods.

And he who treads this lofty land alone,
Will feel, while clouds are round him rent and blown,
    Standing amid the dumb crags, skyward lifting,
A little nearer God's celestial throne.

MOONRISE AT MONTEREY.

ALL through the sultry evening hours
The fluctuant tide's soft swell was heard,
And to the cadence sang a bird
Amid the bright acacia flowers.

A bat zigzagged across the night,
And in the dark the spiders spun
Their webs, that would, at rise of sun,
Be little silvery paths of flight.

Clear notes of song dropped down the air,
Well-rounded, perfect pearls of sound ;
A star sprang eastward, and was drowned
In outer ether, none knew where.

Then, as o'er Latmian leas of yore
She rose to greet Endymion,
Full-orbed and fair the moon outshone
Above the wide Pacific shore.

A SERENADE.

SLUMBER has stilled the note
In the thrush's tender throat ;
But "chirp" the cricket sings,
And the moth's dark wings
Flutter along the night,
Through the pale starlight.
Soft may thine eyelids meet ;
Sleep on, O sweet !

Never a stir 'mid the stars
Of the jasmine at the bars
Of her casement, looking away
Toward the unborn day.
Mount, and an entrance win,
Steal in, my song, steal in !
Soft may thine eyelids meet ;
Sleep on, O sweet !

Steal in, but breathe not above
The lowest whisper of love ;
  Hover around her there
  In that holy air ;
    Glide into her dreams, and be
    A memory of me.
      Soft may thine eyelids meet ;
      Sleep on, O sweet !

THE PRODIGALS.

(*He.*)

LOITERERS, why do ye sit
Where the bees about ye flit
Through the sunlight-goldened hours
In the clover's crimson bowers?
Drowsing in the zephyrs bland,
Lifting ne'er a toiling hand,
Hearing little notes and trills
That the thrush's throat o'erspills,
Happy all the day ye seem,
Half awake and half in dream

(*They.*)

Lying in the leaning grass
Where the lyring crickets pass,
Honey-burdened argosies
Drifting o'er us down the breeze,

Ours it is to never know
Any harbinger of woe,
Any pain that harrieth,
Any haunting fear of death,
But to joy in all around,—
Lustrous light and soothing sound.

(*He.*)

Prithee, how doth it befall
That ye are so prodigal
Of the precious sands of time,
Slipping by in silver chime?
Feel ye not some shame to ne'er
Any task or burden bear?
In the shifting shade and sun
Is there nothing to be won,
That ye still should listless lie
Underneath the arching sky?

(*They.*)

Naught we feel of shame, and naught
Shall there be by any wrought

Who have tasted of the bliss
Of a charmèd life like this.
We have drained the nectar-cup
That the poppy holdeth up,
We have drunk the potent draught
That the lotus-eaters quaffed ;
Careless we whate'er befalls,
Happy-hearted prodigals !

OUR SAINT.

THE one I sing was born and bred
Ere proud Queen Fashion's whims had led
A single maid to vex her head
O'er pug or poodle ;
Her form was lithe, her face was fair,
Her laugh was blithe and debonair,
Her voice was sweet,—her favorite air
Was "Yankee Doodle."

She used to play an old spinet,
The same is in existence yet
Amid the dust and cobwebs set
High in our garret ;
And oft she spun from dawn till gloom
In some quaint, low, be-gabled room ;
She loved the fabric of her loom,
Nor scorned to wear it.

In stately minuet or reel,
With large-bowed slippers, high of heel,
Hers was the step that roused the zeal
In hearts of gallants;
Folk high and lowly both to please,
To make bright *mots* and repartees,
To bake, to brew,—she numbered these
Among her talents.

Whene'er she passed in quilted gown
Along the highways of the town,
Small wonder that the swains bowed down
In admiration;
And when a handsome stranger bore
The fair one from her father's door,
Why marvel that the jealous swore
From sheer vexation?

A day more gay was seldom seen
Than her bright wedding-day, I ween;
And she,—she bore herself a queen
In look and motion.

And when, with him she loved, she led
The wedding-dance, more light her tread
Than any barque that ever sped
O'er wave of ocean.

The broidered bodice that she wore
While footing it along the floor
Has lain for fifty years and more
In some dark chest hid;
And he whose arm around it stole,
Sought while yet young the starry goal,
A grief which she has, patient soul,
Long in her breast hid.

Her eyes are dim, her voice is faint,
And yet she never makes complaint;
One more serene and like a saint
I have to yet see
Than she who in the corner sits
And dozes, while she knits and knits
Her little nephew's socks and mitts,—
My great-aunt Betsy.

IN SOLITUDE.

SOMETIMES at lonely dead of night
  Weird sounds assail the ear,
And in our hearts is cold affright
  To think a ghost is near.

Why should we feel swift through us thrill
  A sense of awe and dread?
It is the living work us ill,
  And not the peaceful dead!

THE BRIC-À-BRAC SHOP.

IT stands within an alley nigh
Where Trade's swift tide goes rolling by;
No sudden sunbeam finds its way
Across the threshold, dusky gray,
But peaceful twilight ever reigns
Behind its dim and dusty panes.
Few are the hands that ope its door;
Few are the feet that tread its floor;
Yet prying folk will sometimes dare
The narrow, dark-walled thoroughfare,
And pause before the sign that shows
That here are "Coins and Curios."

Within the long, low, crowded room
A cheery face makes bright the gloom;
Keen eyes that have a friendly glow
O'er spectacles with silver bow;

A mellow voice, whose gracious phrase
Suggests the courtly olden days.
His wig is always most precise;
His coat and collar always nice;
His parchment volumes, quaint and thin,
Are not more yellow than his skin.
He seems, 'mid tapestry and delf,
A bit of bric-à-brac himself.

In drawer and under carven lid
The choicest treasures he has hid;
Curved blades that bear some mystic sign,
And glass that gleams like amber wine.
But, ah, it is his air and face
That lend a glamour to the place!
Yet from his faltering step we know
That he ere long must surely go,—
That we shall see, as ne'er before,
Some crape upon the dingy door,
And that no kindly voice will cry
"Good-morrow" to the passers-by.

HAREBELLS.

ON the morning breeze to the eager bees
You ring out an elfin chime,
And all day long, while the birds make song,
The spears of the grass keep time.

You ring and you ring till the crickets sing,
And the pale little stars out-flower ;
Till the beetles boom through the purple gloom
Of the odorous twilight hour.

Though your music clear I never may hear,
Yet I know it is sweeter far
Than the mellow flute or the silvery lute,
Or the strains of the viol are.

For that tender blue, your delicate hue,
Was the gift of the arching sky,
And the chimes you ring are the echoing
Of the anthems sung on high.

AN AFRICAN LILY.

WHILE without in riotous din
  The voice of the storm-wind swells,
You proudly uplift within
  Your beautiful scarlet bells.

And the snow-girt landscape fades
  Like a dream from my eyes away,
Till I see palm-sheltered glades
  'Neath the glow of an Afric day.

And there by a languid stream,
  Uncut by the keel of boat,
I seem to behold you gleam
  With a snake twined round your throat.

Still the vision will not flee
  With its spell of baleful power ;—
What awful memory
  Is yours, O beauteous flower?

A ROSE.

ROSE, by fair fingers torn
From off thy thorny stem,
How canst thou droop and mourn
Since so caressed by them?

Better one blissful hour
That opes eternity,
Than length of life for dower
And fail her face to see.

Although 'tis thine to die,
How happy wilt thou rest!
Thy requiem her sigh,
Thy tomb her peaceful breast.

A WINTER TWILIGHT.

THE silent snowflakes glance and gleam
  Adown the chilly Northern air ;
The West has thrown its dying beam
  Athwart the forest gray and bare.

And now a gradual dimness veils
  The wintry landscape near and far,
And while the windy daylight pales
  Out-glimmers clear a single star.

Lulled by the sound of tinkling strings
  Where nimble fingers weave their spell,
I quite forget the North that stings
  Without the cozy oriel.

And on the wings of music borne,
  Aglow with floods of gold, I see
The blue of skies that rarely mourn
  Arch o'er the slopes of Italy.

The melody seems wafted down
  From laurelled heights where roses blow,
That shimmer like an emerald crown
  Above embowered Bellaggio.

A molten sapphire Como lies,
  And opal sails across it skim ;
Green stair on stair the mountains rise,
  And cut the calm horizon's rim.

All dims as dies the rapturing strain ;
  Once more the deepening dusk I see ;
Then strike the silent chords again,
  That I may dream of Italy !

MELLONA.

TELL me, thou that watchest o'er
Gatherers of golden honey
Through the tranquil days and sunny,
Days that now we see no more,
Where have fled those toilers belted
With refulgent bands of amber?
Leafless are the vines that clamber
Where they revel held of yore.
Filched the rare ambrosia melted
In the honeysuckle bells;
Drained the nectar from the cells
Of the zenith-looking lily;
While the winds through wan and chilly
Hours around us rage and roar.
They have robbed the year of sweetness,
Leaving us its ashen core;
Have they followed thee with fleetness

Holding still their wealth in store?
In our visions we behold,—
While the stinging storm-shafts hurtle
O'er the buried beds of myrtle,—
All thy honey's liquid gold,
Drained from asphodels of old
Where Arcadian fountains spurtle.
Cruel, cruel, thus to flaunt us
Through the chill of wintry night!
Cruel, cruel, thus to haunt us
With sweet visions of delight!
Come, we pray thee, come and bring
Back thy troop, and sky-fields sunny;
We would quaff the year's fresh honey
From the chalice of the Spring!

IN THE PARK.

SITTING within a grassy, tree-girt park,
I heard a mocking bird whose glad songs mark
The hours from radiant dawn to purple dark.

The air was sweet with fragrance, blossom-born ;
Nature was joyous as the east at morn,
And blushed from peach-tree bough and leafy thorn.

Like tall, slim maidens in an emerald wood,
Amid the grasses stately tulips stood,
With here a damask, there an amber hood.

A fountain plashed and murmured low near by,
Athwart whose jets shone rays as bright of dye
As those that span a tempest-clearing sky.

Light-footed children danced in shade and sun,
Lithe-limbed as fawns that through dim coverts run
At crimson dawning when the night is done.

It was a pleasant spot to dream away
The hours that hasted toward the dusk of day,
To dream of seasons gone,—where, none may say.

There came a vision to my drowsy brain ;
I thought my buoyant footsteps trod again
A boundless waste of Arizonian plain.

I saw pine-crested mountains grandly rise
To clasp the quivering blue of cloudless skies,
As if ambitious of some high emprise.

I heard the tinkling of a burro's bell
Sound through the gulches, green with chapparal,
Far borne on winds that softly rose and fell.

Along the plaza of a Mexic town
I wandered 'twixt bare walls sun-lit and brown,
A modern cavalier without renown.

The strange scene vanished: soft the fountain played;
The children frolicked in the sun and shade;
A willow bowed its head as though it prayed.

Amid the beauties of that tranquil day,
What subtle hint was given, who shall say,
Of flights unburdened by this cloak of clay?

NIGHTFALL.

THE fading rays of daylight slant
  Across the flower-set garden way,
The robins in the maples chant
  The requiem of day.

A single star within the west
  Upon the breast of evening lies,
While like a spectre of unrest
  The scarred moon mounts the skies.

And by a casement wide apart
  Through which the night wind wandereth,
A watcher ponders in his heart
  The mystery of death.

A DREAM OF PEACE.

I.

I HEARD a clear voice clarion, "War is o'er,"
  And joyful tongues replied, "Want is no more!"
Was it in dreamland, or that border-land
    Between the realms of sleep and consciousness?
      Now that wide-waking I walk forth abroad,
      I hear heart-piercing prayers mount up to God,
    That in his pity he may bend and bless
    The needy many in their sore distress;
That he may hold to them a helping hand
Lest in their weakness and their woe they fall;
And with the prayers I hear the mingled call
Of awful curses rise beside the way;
"There is no God, there is no God," they say.
"Would a just Lord allow us all our lives
    In misery to toil and struggle here?
To swarm together in low human hives?

To huddle close as does the stolid brute,
No brightening ray of joy dark year on year,
No pleasant plucking of life's golden fruit,
But dreary plodding from sad sun to sun
Until our wretched span of days is done?"

II.

Where'er I pass upleaps the bitter cry,
And the land hears it and the o'erleaning sky.
Ah! is it not an antique burden borne
Along dim vistas of unnumbered years;
Had it not birth within the outraged breast
Of those afflicted, goaded and oppressed
When earth was young among her sister spheres,
Not hoar with ruin such as Rome uprears?
There must be ever those who weep and mourn
For the lost looks of dear death-slumbering eyes,
But must there ever sound these piteous cries,
These curses that affright the timid air?
Where is the respite from the old despair
Now that the time of tyrants is no more?
(Or rules there still a despot hand afar

Where swollen Neva frets an ice-bound shore,
And pallid exiles in bleak Asia pine
Because they bowed not to the great White Czar ?)
Will man ne'er build a universal shrine
To pure-souled Peace in any coming age,
When cruel War and Want no longer rage ?

III.

Alas ! for Peace while daily to and fro
The deadly-armed, alert battalions go,
In those old lands whose fields the soldier's blood
Has riched for harvest with its crimson tide ;
What Peace is there where men may leap at call
To bristling Battle's devastating brawl,
Save in a name for scoffers to deride ?
Not ours to see the altars sanctified !
Again must flow the sacrificial flood,
Again must Carnage strike a clangorous peal,
Again must ring and flash the burnished steel,
And hearths and homes and hearts be desolate !
Not till the demons Avarice and Hate
Are held within a tighter leash than now,

Not until Freedom has a wider scope
Will white Peace-shrines be wreathed with olive-bough,
Nor spectral Want that strides in wake of War
Be driven from the last land's furthest slope.
Love, Love will be the bloodless conqueror
If e'er the dreamed-of, blissful reign have birth,—
Harmonious heaven on a strifeless earth.

IV.

Shall we then let Hope's helpful beacon die,
Albeit we hear the curses and the cry
Of hunger rise around us, and well know
That unborn daisies on sun-ambered hills
Must redden with irreparable stain?
If Faith abides, some high immortal gain
Will shine through clouds that shroud the sorest ills;
But it is Hope, enduring Hope that fills
And stirs the breast with the divinest glow.
Slow are the secret alchemies that bring
The lily to its flowerful perfecting.
May not the gradual change of Nature's plan
Unfold the process of the change of man?

Naught is achieved by one stupendous bound ;
  The bud, the flower, the fruit, each has its time !
Some distant day may not the clarion sound
   That clamored out of dreamland, "War is o'er,"
  Till mountains skyward lift the song sublime,
   And seas repeat it loud from shore to shore ?
Hope, burning brightly o'er the Future's gate,
Bids us a little longer, "Watch and wait !"

www.ingramcontent.com/pod-product-compliance
Lightning Source LLC
LaVergne TN
LVHW011231110826
845150LV00006B/1609

* 9 7 8 1 4 2 5 5 1 4 4 7 1 *